Baby Hummingbirds

A True Story

By Mary Haring Purvis

Copyright © 2016 By Mary Haring Purvis.

All rights reserved. No part of this book may be used or reproduced by any means, graphic, electronic, or mechanical, including photocopying, recording, taping or by any information storage retrieval system without the written permission of the author except in the case of brief quotations embodied in critical articles and reviews.

This book is a work of non-fiction. Unless otherwise noted, the author and the publisher make no explicit guarantees as to the accuracy of the information contained in this book and in some cases, names of people and places have been altered to protect their privacy.

Scripture taken from the Holy Bible, NEW INTERNATIONAL VERSION®. Copyright © 1973, 1978, 1984, 2011 by Biblica, Inc. All rights reserved worldwide. Used by permission. NEW INTERNATIONAL VERSION® and NIV® are registered trademarks of Biblica, Inc. Use of either trademark for the offering of goods or services requires the prior written consent of Biblica US, Inc.

WestBow Press books may be ordered through booksellers or by contacting:

WestBow Press
A Division of Thomas Nelson & Zondervan
1663 Liberty Drive
Bloomington, IN 47403
www.westbowpress.com
1 (866) 928-1240

Because of the dynamic nature of the Internet, any web addresses or links contained in this book may have changed since publication and may no longer be valid. The views expressed in this work are solely those of the author and do not necessarily reflect the views of the publisher, and the publisher hereby disclaims any responsibility for them.

Any people depicted in stock imagery provided by Thinkstock are models, and such images are being used for illustrative purposes only.
Certain stock imagery © Thinkstock.

ISBN: 978-1-5127-4756-0 (sc)
ISBN: 978-1-5127-4757-7 (e)

Library of Congress Control Number: 2016910424

Print information available on the last page.

WestBow Press rev. date: 07/02/2016

Baby Hummingbirds
A True Story

Is lovingly dedicated

To my precious grandchildren

Marianna Rose

Kayleigh Elizabeth

Russell Andrew III

Amelia Marie

Matthew James

Ramsey Omar

Johnathan Craig

And all future grandbabies!

Once upon a time, in a country far, far away, there lived two tiny baby hummingbirds in a big, big tree. Mommy hummingbird spent her days bringing sweet flower nectar for her babies to eat. They were very cozy and very happy together.

Then one day, *men* came to chop down the tree. They were not bad men. They didn't even know the hummingbird family lived in the tree.

Chop, chop, chop. Crash! Boom! Bang!

The big branches fell to the ground. The baby hummingbirds held on to the little nest with all their might.

A kind lady found the nest with the two baby birdies safe inside. Mommy hummingbird was nowhere to be found. The kind lady made homemade nectar to feed the baby hummingbirds.

Hummingbirds are the smallest birds in the whole world.

The days passed. The kind lady took good care of the babies. She named them *The Twins*. She caught fresh flies and fed them to the baby hummingbirds along with the sweet nectar.

Before long, only one baby birdie fit in the nest, and her brother perched on the edge of the nest as if standing guard.

Sometimes they would flutter their little wings very hard and try to fly. But not yet baby birdies.

The Twins were growing rapidly. They no longer fit in their walnut-size nest.

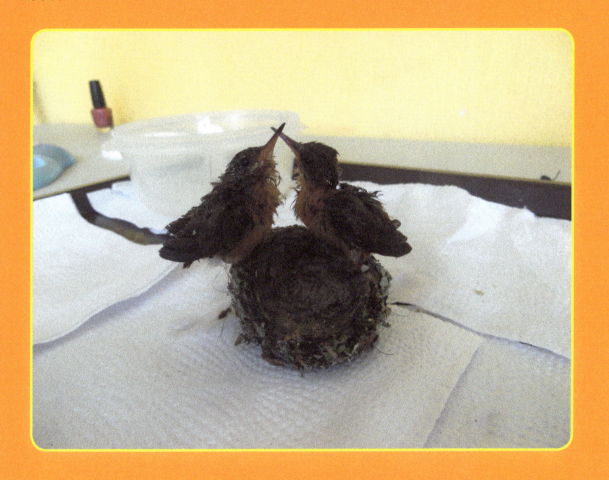

Using small branches from the big, big tree that had been chopped down, the kind lady made a special habitat for *The Twins*.

She made a hummingbird feeder out of an old syrup bottle. *The Twins* learned to drink on their own.

Each day the kind lady put a new banana peeling in the habitat. That attracted fruit flies and the babies learned to eat them using their fast little tongues. They were happy and safe.

But still….. *The Twins* missed their Mommy.

Lots of people came, from near and far, to visit *The Twins*.

Visitors would hold them,

and talk to them,

and love them…

…and even laugh with them.

The babies didn't mind the attention at all. They loved their habitat, they loved the visitors, and they loved the soft, lined basket they slept in at night, safe inside the kind lady's bedroom.

Then one day, something amazing happened!

"What was that?"

Mommy hummingbird found her babies!

The Twins could not believe their eyes!

Mommy hummingbird flitted and fluttered and danced with joy at finding her babies safe and sound!

What a happy reunion!

Most birds won't come back to their babies if a human touches them. BUT, a mommy hummingbird will.

Mommy hummingbird quickly took over the task of feeding her babies. She would dash away. Soon she would return, stick her beak inside one of the baby's mouths, and drop a tasty morsel inside.

The Twins were delighted to have their Mommy back. Mommy hummingbird was happy that her babies were ok. She spent hours chattering with them. They listened intently.

Mommy hummingbird began to teach the baby hummingbirds how to fly. Day after day she worked with *The Twins* and showed them just how to flutter their little wings up to 70 times per second.

Hummingbirds do not flap their wings, but rather they rotate them in a figure 8. That way, they can go backwards in the air and even hover in one spot like a little helicopter. *The Twins* were learning to fly!

Then suddenly, one morning when the kind lady looked for the hummingbird family, they were gone.

Mommy hummingbird had taken them to the new, safe nest that she had built for them, high up in another big tree. Every day, they would return to the kind lady's house to sip nectar out of her colorful flowers.

And they all lived happily, ever after.

THE END

TEACHABLE MOMENT

Matthew 10:29-31 (NIV)

Are not two sparrows sold for a penny? Yet not one of them will fall to the ground outside your Father's care. And even the very hairs of your head are all numbered. So don't be afraid; you are worth more than many sparrows.

ABOUT THE AUTHOR

Mary Haring Purvis grew up as a missionary kid in a Tarascan Indian village in Mexico. Now she is a missionary herself in a Maya-Achi Indian village in Guatemala. *Baby Hummingbirds* is a true story based on what happened to Ms. Purvis while living in Guatemala. All the pictures are originals of this unique experience.

Ms. Purvis, (aka "*the kind lady*"), has four children and seven grandchildren who all live in the United States of America.

To contact the author, or to learn more about her ministry in Guatemala, please see:

Email: corazonmhp@hotmail.com

Website: www.GuatemalaLandingZone.com

Facebook page: www.facebook.com/GuatemalaLandingZone